GW00670997

THE OFFICIAL
NOTTINGHAM
FOREST FC
ANNUAL 2012

FOREST

Contributors: John Lawson, Fraser Nicholson, Ben White, Jonathon Ogle, Cheryl McCluskey
Designed by Cavan Convery

A Grange Publication

© 2011. Published by Grange Communications Ltd., Edinburgh under licence from Nottingham Forest Football Club. Printed in the EU.

Photography © Action Images, Press Association Images, John Sumpter Photography and Geoff Peabody.

ISBN   978-1-908221-48-3

£7.99

CONTENTS

NEW SIGNINGS

FOREST

GEORGE BOATENG

JONATHAN GREENING

ANDY REID

Steve McClaren set his sights on adding experience and striking power to his Nottingham Forest side when taking over at The City Ground last summer.

And after much hard work in the transfer markel he achieved just that in his first two months in the job.

In doing so he also brought a Forest favourite back to familiar surroundings when he signed Republic of Ireland midfielder Andy Reid after his contract with Blackpool had expired.

He moved on from there to capture Jonathan Greening from Fulham and then made it a trio of midfield signings when George Boateng, a player he knew well from his successful days at Middlesbrough, agreed to move to Trentside after a year in Greek football.

The new manager then turned his attentions to his strike force by agreeing a deal with Matt Derbyshire after the former Blackburn goalscorer had come to the end of his spell in Greece with Olympiakos.

And the signings continued when West Brom hit man Ishmael Miller was persuaded to make the move across the Midlands in an initial £1.2m transfer.

Said McClaren: "Before I arrived at the club so

MATT DERBYSHIRE

ISHMAEL MILLER

many players had left following the end of last season and there was a need to bring in new faces.

"We identified straight away that we required players with more experience. I took over a very talented group of players when I arrived at Forest but there was a youthfulness about them that had to be balanced out by recruiting players with vital experience

"With the signings of Andy, Jonathan and George we did that but it was also clear that we had to sign players who carried an attacking threat because, in our opening matches of the season, we were not posing enough problems for the opposition defence.

"Matt ticked all the boxes for us. He's only 25 but he's had good experience in the game, has played in the Premier League and has had the benefits of figuring in European football during his time in Greece.

"At 24, Ishmael is also still young but has loads of experience and lots to prove. He wants to play regular football and we can provide the platform for him to do that.

"He's ambitious and fits our criteria perfectly. The opportunity is now there for him and Matt to strike up a partnership and also go from strength to strength as individuals."

FOREST LEGEND

STUART PEARCE

It wasn't difficult to understand why Stuart Pearce earned legendary status with our fans in the 80s and 90s.

The man our fans christened 'Psycho', was an inspirational figure in a City Ground career that spanned 12 years, 522 games and 88 goals.

His drive and determination were a feature of our performances throughout that time and his leadership qualities were second to none as he lifted Brian Clough's rebuilt side to new heights.

Crunching tackles were his trademark. So too were the rampaging forward runs that brought him an incredible supply of goals from full-back.

He helped us win the League Cup twice during his time at The City Ground – in 1989 and 1990 – and was so close to leading us to the FA Cup success in 1991 when we lost in the final to Tottenham Hotspur.

Towards the end of his Forest career as a player he also acted as caretaker-manager before eventually leaving to extend his life as a full-back with Newcastle, West Ham and Manchester City.

His love of representing England was well-known and he played 78 times for his country and captained them on ten occasions.

When his playing days finally ended, he managed Manchester City from 2005-07 and has since been in charge of the England Under-21 squad.

MANAGER STEVE McCLAREN

Steve McClaren says there were a few surprises waiting for him when he took over as manager of Nottingham Forest.

McClaren was appointed at The City Ground in June 2011 and, helped by people who were already at the club, settled very quickly to life in Nottingham.

He said: "I was very pleasantly surprised by the quality of the people that were at the club already.

"Yes, we are trying to build a successful team on the field but getting things right off the field is very important as well.

"Everyone works together and we all want the same things.

"They helped my staff and myself feel settled and comfortable at the club."

The appointment of McClaren captured the imagination of not only Forest's fans but also the football world in general, as it represented his first job in this

country since his spell as England manager.

He finished working with the Three Lions in 2008 but went on to enjoy great success in Holland with FC Twente.

They won the Dutch title for the first time in their history under McClaren and after a spell in Germany with Wolfsburg he decided the time was right to return to England where he enjoyed great success in club management with Middlesbrough.

After a spell as assistant manager to Sir Alex Ferguson at Manchester United, he led Boro to the 2004 League Cup – the first trophy they had ever won – and two years later took them all the way to the final of the UEFA Cup.

He helped England manager Sven-Goran Eriksson at the 2006 World Cup and took over from him after the tournament.

As a player, McClaren served Hull, Derby County, Bristol City and Oxford United before starting his coaching career with Derby.

HONOURS BOARD

Football League

Division One
Champions 1977-78 and 1997-98
Runners-up 1966-67 and 1978-79

Division Two
Champions 1906-07 and 1921-22
Runners-up 1956-57

League One
Runners-up 2007-08

Division Three (South)
Champions 1950-51

F.A. Cup
Winners 1898 and 1959
Runners-up 1991

Football League Cup
Winners 1978, 1979, 1989 and 1990
Runners-up 1980 and 1982

European Cup
Winners 1979 and 1980

European Super Cup
Winners 1979-80
Runners-up 1980-81

Simod Cup
Winners 1989

Zenith Data Systems Cup
Winners 1992

Anglo-Scottish Cup
Winners 1977

Charity Shield
Winners 1978

WHICH PERSON OUTSIDE OF FOOTBALL?

I would have to say my dad, especially when I was in my early teens and it would have been quite easy to lose my focus.

I've lost count of the number of lads who showed a great deal of promise fade away from football because they didn't have the right guidance, someone to show them right from wrong.

I was fortunate that I had my dad behind me. He was a little bit strict at times but I can't complain because I'm living out my dream.

WHICH COACH?

Eric Steele was goalkeeping coach at Derby and when I was 12 or 13 he took me to one side and said he thought I had something about me.

I think a few other coaches were having doubts about me but Eric really stood up for me and fought my corner.

I'm relatively small for a 'keeper but it was even more the case when I was a kid and a lot of people wrote me off because of that.

But Eric told me that if I kept working hard I stood a chance of making it and fortunately he was right. I call him 'The Guru' when I speak to him and I'll always be grateful for his guidance and support.

WHICH FAMOUS PERSON?

When I was 15 or 16 I worked closely with Derby's No.1 Mart Poom, who was in my opinion among the top three goalkeepers in the Premier League at the time.

He was a fantastic professional and although he didn't do a lot wrong I probably learnt more from the few mistakes he did make.

He trained too hard at times and really pushed his body to the limit and although he got results because of that he also struggled with a couple of injuries, which could have been avoided.

But it worked and getting the opportunity to learn alongside him was a real privilege.

WHICH SONG?

There's not a particular song but I do listen to a particular album before games – it's an 80's soul compilation and I listen to it on the team bus.

I can't remember who we were playing when I first listened to it before a game but we won that day and I've listened to it ever since. It's a superstition of mine.

WHICH FILM?

I really like 'Remember the Titans' which is based around American football. Two schools integrate and it tells the story of how people overcame racial prejudice. It's a really compelling story.

WHO AM I?

Morgan

Tudgay

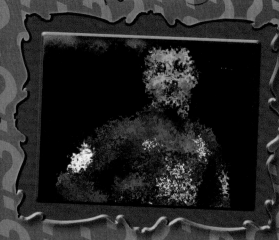

My Forest debut was against Crystal Palace.
I was born in 1983.
I was Sheffield Wednesday's top goal-scorer last season.
I came here on emergency loan.
I am 175cm tall.
I also used to play for Derby County.

My Forest debut was against Port Vale.
I was born in 1984.
I played 51 games for Forest last season.
I scored 3 goals last season.
I am 185cm tall.
I have also played for Kidderminster (on loan).

My Forest debut was against Bradford City.
I was born in 1985.
I used to play for Northampton Town.
I'm a reliable defender.
I am 185cm tall.
I've also been known to score a few goals.

My Forest debut was against Carlisle.
I was born in 1987.
I was offered a trial at The City Ground by fomer manager Colin Calderwood.
I'm a pacey winger known for my tricks.
I am 180cm tall.
I joined Forest from non-league Bromley.

Answers on page 60

LEE WESTWOOD

Golf ace Lee Westwood OBE has another sporting passion – Nottingham Forest.

Lee hails from north Nottinghamshire and is an avid supporter of The Reds who tries to get along to games at The City Ground as often as his golfing commitments allow him.

Such is his love for Forest that he has even been known to wear the red and white when he plays in major tournaments around the world.

"Wherever I am in the world I manage to keep in touch with what's going on at The City Ground," he says.

"Loads of the other British lads on the golf tour follow football teams so there's always a lot of banter flying about."

Other celebrity Forest fans include James Dean Bradfield, who is the lead singer of 'The Manic Street Preachers', Chris Urbanowicz from the band 'The Editors', Emmerdale actor James Hooton and England cricket star Stuart Broad.

The fast bowler reveals: "I love coming to games at The City Ground.

"I don't get the chance to get down to Forest a huge amount because we're obviously playing away a lot in the winter.

"But when I do come down I always find the atmosphere to be brilliant and I love the style of play."

Urbanowicz adds: "My parents are from Nottingham, I was born in Nottingham and my dad is a Forest fan... so I didn't have much choice really.

"I used to go and watch them when I could. I was eight or nine when I watched my first game at The City Ground when we drew with QPR.

"That was good but I had a headache. I was a bit of a sick boy when I was a kid and used to get headaches all the time... but it didn't stop me enjoying the game. It was still an amazing experience.

"Stuart Pearce would have to be my favourite ever player but when I was a kid my head teacher at primary school compared me to a young Nigel Clough because I used to play in his position. So he was a big favourite of mine, along with Gary Crosby.

"I've never met any of the Forest players because people in the football and rock and roll worlds seem to move in different circles – they don't seem to overlap that much which might surprise a few people."

FOREST FACTS

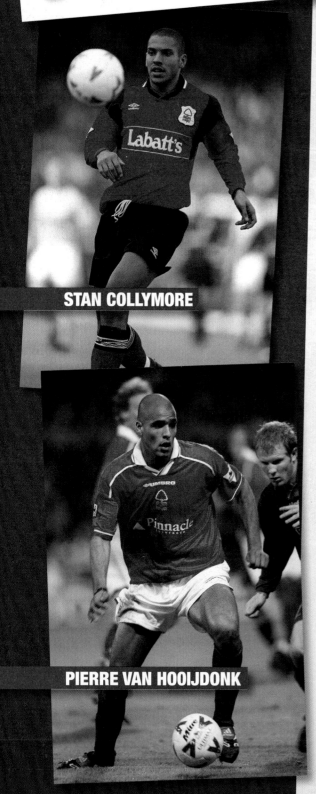

STAN COLLYMORE

PIERRE VAN HOOIJDONK

EARLY DAYS...

We are one of the oldest football clubs in England, having been formed in 1865 by a group of shinty players.

Shinty is a form of hockey, which these days is mainly played in the Scottish Highlands.

RECORD FEE RECEIVED

The biggest transfer fee we have received for a player was £8.5m from Liverpool for goal king Stan Collymore in June 1995.

PRICEY PIERRE

Dutch international striker Pierre van Hooijdonk is still our record signing. It cost us £3.5m to buy him from Glasgow Celtic in March 1997.

YOUNG GUN

Our youngest ever player was Craig Westcarr, who was just 16 years and 257 days old when he played against Burnley in October 2001.

EURO EARNER

The record receipts at The City Ground were for a UEFA Cup quarter-final tie against top German side Bayern Munich in March 1996.

STAR STRIKER

Ace striker Tom Peacock scored four goals in a match for us four times in the 1930s.

CAP THAT!

Our most capped player is Stuart Pearce, who represented England 76 times during his time at The City Ground.

RECORD GATE

Our record attendance at The City Ground is 49,946 against Manchester United in October 1967.

BIGGEST VICTORY

Our record league victory is a 12-0 goalrush against Leicester Fosse way back in April 1909.

But we went two better than that in an FA Cup game in 1891 when we defeated Clapton 14-0!

MILLION POUND MAN

We were the first club to pay £1m for a player when Trevor Francis arrived at The City Ground from Birmingham City in February 1979.

PIONEER VIV

Our former full-back Viv Anderson was the first black player to represent England when he played against Czechoslovakia at Wembley in 1978.

Viv also holds another record – he has played the most games for us in European football (32).

FIRST WITH SHIN PADS

We were the first team to wear shin pads after they were invented by one of our players Sam Widdowson in 1874.

INTRODUCING GOAL NETS

We were involved in the introduction of crossbar and nets to football.

They came into the game in 1891, invented by a Liverpool man James Brodie, and the first trial of them was on the Forest ground for a match between the North and the South.

Before then the goal had been two uprights with a ribbon or tape across the top.

FLOODED OUT!

In the winter of 1946-47 the weather was so bad that The City Ground pitch was flooded almost to the height of the crossbars.

FOREST ON FIRE!

There was a big fire at The City Ground on August 24 1968 when a match between ourselves and Leeds United had to be abandoned.

The Main Stand was completely destroyed and while it was being rebuilt we played our home games at Notts County's ground Meadow Lane.

SAME AGAIN… AND AGAIN

When Forest won the FA Cup by beating Luton Town 2-1 in 1959 the same eleven players figured in every one of the ties leading up to and including the final.

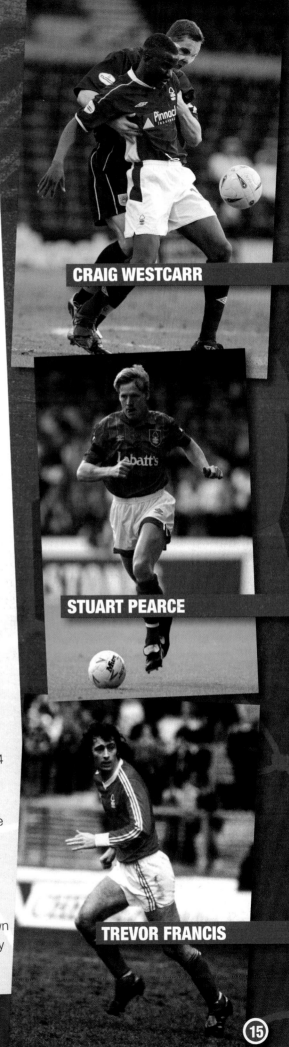

CRAIG WESTCARR

STUART PEARCE

TREVOR FRANCIS

How much do you know about the Super Reds?

Here's your chance to test your knowledge in our big Forest Quiz. You can find out how many you got right by turning to page 60 for the answers. Good luck!

1 Who was our top goalscorer in all competitions last season?

2 From which club did we sign Chris Gunter?

3 Who is our longest serving player?

4 Which of our former players has managed Leicester, Celtic and Aston Villa?

5 Who was our manager the last time we won promotion to the Premier League in 1997-98?

6 Who were our only ever-present players in Championship games last season?

7 Who scored our goals when we defeated Derby County 5-2 last season?

R. Earnshaw

8 Who was the other Forest player who left The City Ground alongside Michael Dawson for Tottenham in 2005?

9 Can you name our former striker who won promotion from League Two with Chesterfield last season?

10 Which club did our goalkeeper Paul Smith join on loan during last season?

11 We finished sixth in the Championship last season. Can you name the top five in order?

12 From which American club did we sign World Cup striker Robbie Findley during last season?

13 What was the Brian Clough Stand at The City Ground previously known as?

14 Which team defeated us in the League One play-offs at the end of the 2006-07 season?

15 And which current Forest player lined up against us in those games?

16 Can you name Paul Anderson's previous clubs?

17 Who scored our first Championship goal last season?

18 At which club did Marcus Tudgay start his professional career?

19 How many years was manager Brian Clough in charge at The City Ground?

20 Who scored our goals when we lost 3-2 to West Ham at Upton Park in the third round of last season's FA Cup?

MY INSPIRATIONS
CHRIS GUNTER

WHICH COACH AS A YOUNG PLAYER?

There were two coaches who were really influential, Terry Moore and John Kerr.

Terry worked with me at Cardiff from Under-13s until I left school. He played a massive part in my early development and I still speak to him on occasions now.

I then became a full-time scholar at Cardiff and worked with John, who was Academy Director as well as a coach.

He was brilliant and it was a real shock when, after my first year as a scholar, he sadly passed away.

WHICH BOOK?

I've read a few autobiographies but Peter Schmeichel's is the best I've read. Before I started playing I wanted to be a goalkeeper and had all the shirts and Schmeichel was a favourite of mine.

He was the best goalkeeper of his generation.

WHICH SONG?

I went through a phase of having to listen to the same music on my ipod on the team bus before every game.

There were quite a few and how long I listened to each song would depend on the length of the journey.

I got it into my head that I had to listen to a bit of each song... so if it was only a short bus ride I would have a quick blast of each one. It used to drive me mad.

It was a real mix of music and included the Arctic Monkeys and a load of dance songs.

I started it when I was at Tottenham – or possibly even before I joined them – but have stopped doing it now.

WHICH FILM?

My favourite films are the Bourne trilogy, especially the first two which are fantastic.

WHICH FAMOUS PERSON?

I suppose as a Welshman I would have to say Ryan Giggs because he has been at the top of the game for so long.

And to actually get the chance to play alongside him in one of his last games for Wales was a massive honour for me.

FOREST LEGEND

PETER SHILTON

Peter Shilton was one of the greatest goalkeepers of all time… and he had an amazing career in the game spanning more than three decades.

But his most successful time was undoubtedly spent at The City Ground, helping us to double European glory as well as a host of other domestic trophies.

He had already played around 400 of his 1,005 league games with Leicester City and Stoke City before being signed by Brian Clough for us in 1977.

The fee was £300,000 and most people at the time thought it was too much money for a goalkeeper but Shilton went on to prove otherwise.

He joined us in the early weeks of our First Division Championship campaign and his brilliant goalkeeping went on to play a huge part in us lifting the title that year.

He was our last line of defence for five magnificent seasons as we continued to be one of the major forces in the game. Then he moved on to Southampton and had a lengthy spell with our arch-rivals Derby County before having brief spells with a number of other clubs.

But he will always be remembered for his superb displays for us that won him his first major medals in the game.

He also represented England on no fewer than 125 occasions at senior level – a fantastic record by a fantastic goalkeeper.

SEASON REVIEW 2010-11

FOREST

AUGUST

August started on a bright note just before the new season kicked off, as we secured the services of Ryan Bertrand from Chelsea on a six-month loan deal to become our sole signing of the summer.

The left-back went straight into our side for the first match of the new campaign away at Burnley, which unfortunately saw us finish on the wrong side of a 1-0 scoreline after big striker Chris Iwelumo netted for the Clarets.

Despite the defeat, the performance was pleasing and gave many fans optimism of a promotion push come May.

However, the rest of the month continued in the slow fashion of the season opener, as we drew our remaining three league games of the month.

Before our next league action though, we crashed out of the Carling Cup against Bradford City, despite taking the lead through Matt Thornhill.

The midfielder's first-half goal was overturned and the Bantams ran out 2-1 winners in Yorkshire.

Back to the league fixtures, and home draws against newly-promoted Leeds United and Norwich City came either side of a stalemate against Reading at The

Madejski Stadium, with all three games finishing as 1-1 draws.

The Leeds game was really a 'game of two halves', as we hammered at the Leeds' door in the first half and deservedly took the lead through Dexter Blackstock.

However Simon Grayson's men hit back through Lloyd Sam and the second half turned into a scrappy affair, with both sets of fans admitting a draw was probably a fair result.

Blackstock added to his tally with another strike in the game against Norwich, whilst Robert Earnshaw got himself off the mark away at Reading with one of the most extraordinary goals you will ever see.

The Welsh striker pounced on a mistake from Reading keeper Adam Federici, who had kicked the ball against a Reading defender, and Earnshaw rolled the ball into an empty net to cancel out Alex Pearce's opener for the Royals.

Said Earnshaw: "It was bizarre, I didn't know what was happening!

"But I think if anyone deserves a bit of luck from the last few games then I think it is me and I'll take any goal."

SEPTEMBER

We entered September with the task of entertaining yet another newly-promoted side at The City Ground in the shape of Millwall.

Kenny Jackett's men got off to the best possible start when they scored after just four minutes through striker Steve Morison.

We then got the perfect chance to level soon after, as Nathan Tyson was brought down in the box and the referee had little hesitation in awarding us a penalty.

Leading scorer Dexter Blackstock stepped up but the striker blazed his spot-kick high over the bar.

Despite this, we battled on and got a deserved equaliser ten minutes from time, with Blackstock making amends for his penalty miss by heading home a deep Chris Cohen cross.

Our first win of the season came in the following game when we fought from a goal down to win 2-1 against Preston North End.

Lewis McGugan bagged both the goals at Deepdale to see us claim our first three points of the season.

Another away trip followed, as we took on recently-relegated Hull City live on SKY.

Despite a battling performance we couldn't find a breakthrough in a goalless draw.

Luke Chambers had our best chance of the game, while Lee Camp kept us level with a fine save from Jimmy Bullard.

We ended the month with consecutive home games against Swansea City and Sheffield United.

McGugan helped himself to another two goals against the Swans, with Radoslaw Majewski also finding the net in a 3-1 win.

We had to settle for a draw in our final game of the month, however, against the Blades with captain Paul McKenna cancelling out Richard Cresswell's sixth-minute opener for United as the game finished 1-1.

Midfielder McGugan seemed happy enough with his prolonged run in the side and was confident of remaining a fixture in the team.

He said: "I think this year it is just a case of knuckling down and when you get your chances to try and take them.

"Thankfully I have done that but it has only been three games and I want to be a vital part of the team throughout the whole season. I want to build on this."

OCTOBER

Sitting in eleventh place as we moved into October, we found ourselves making consecutive trips to Yorkshire after the international break to face Doncaster Rovers and then Barnsley.

We managed to claim a creditable draw from our trip to the Keepmoat Stadium, despite being unable to hold on to our first-half lead.

Dexter Blackstock added to his season's tally by scoring from close range before Rovers' Adam Lockwood responded almost immediately and drew the home side level.

Our next trip to Yorkshire, however, was one to forget as we crashed to a 3-1 defeat to Barnsley at Oakwell.

Goals from Nathan Doyle

NOVEMBER

The month of November was overshadowed by the injury picked up by popular striker Dexter Blackstock against Cardiff City, midway through the month, which would rule him out for the rest of the season.

Blackstock ruptured his knee ligaments in a collision with Cardiff's Seyi Olofinjana, not long after he had come off the bench to net our second goal in the 2-0 win over the Welshmen.

Before that fantastic win against Cardiff, we had put together a mini unbeaten run, having taken two draws and a win in the games previous.

We claimed a hard-fought away point against Watford at Vicarage Road with Lewis McGugan scoring yet another screamer to bring us level after Jordan Mutch had opened the scoring early on for the Hornets.

Coventry City were next up and we again came from behind… but this time to win the game.

After Luke Chambers scored an unfortunate own-goal to put the Sky Blues in front, we hit back through midfielders Radoslaw Majewski and Chris Cohen to ensure that the three points were ours.

Table-topping QPR were the next team to visit The City Ground and they proved to be a stern test for us.

A smart save by Lee Camp from Adel Taarabt ensured he kept a clean sheet and although we couldn't find a breakthrough ourselves, it had to be seen as a well-earned point against the league leaders.

We received a massive boost towards the end of the month by bringing in two new loan signings.

Striker Marcus Tudgay checked in from Sheffield Wednesday, while Arsenal star Aaron Ramsey also signed, in order to gain match fitness since recovering from his broken leg.

Both men were in the squad for our trip to the

and former Red Andy Gray gave the Tykes a two-goal lead before Lewis McGugan brought us back into the game.

Yet our hopes of snatching a point were dashed three minutes from time as Jacob Butterfield scored a third for Barnsley.

We got back to winning ways against Middlesbrough just three days later as yet another stunning McGugan strike was enough to see off Boro in a 1-0 win.

This result was then followed up by another home win, this time at the expense of Roy Keane's Ipswich Town.

David McGoldrick made a rare start in attack and he responded by firing us in front before a spectacular free-kick from McGugan completed the win with a strike destined to be a contender for goal of the season.

We finished the month with a long trip to the south coast to take on Portsmouth and the 2-1 defeat summed up an 'up and down' month for Billy Davies's men as Paul Anderson's goal was in vain as again we lost on the road.

Walkers Stadium in the first East Midlands derby of the season but were unable to stop Leicester beating us 1-0 thanks to an Andy King strike.

Cohen, on scoring his first goal of the season against Coventry, said: "It's quite funny actually because the gaffer had a £20 bet with 'Earnie' that I would score and I told the gaffer not to waste his money!"

DECEMBER

The cold snap really affected us in December with several postponed fixtures.

Our games against Bristol City (home) and Scunthorpe United and Middlesbrough (both away) were affected by the Arctic conditions and eventually fell foul of the weather.

For many of the players it was a welcome rest but for new recruits Aaron Ramsey and Marcus Tudgay it became a frustrating period as they were itching to get their Forest careers started.

We did manage to squeeze in two games at The City Ground either side of Christmas, firstly sweeping aside Crystal Palace 3-0 which included a debut goal for new boy Tudgay.

Luke Chambers started the scoring, heading home from a Lewis McGugan corner.

The second half was barely a minute old before Tudgay raced onto a long ball forward by Guy Moussi and confidently lobbed over the stranded Julian Speroni in the Palace goal.

Garath McCleary put the finishing touches to the win, with a driven strike five minutes from time that left Speroni with no chance.

We ended 2010 in the best possible fashion, by beating rivals Derby County 5-2 and in doing so

inflicted our biggest ever win over the Rams for 100 years.

We started brightly and the in-form Chambers headed us in front after two minutes from a Radi Majewski corner before Luke Moore equalised for Derby.

However, a Tudgay double, against his former club, put us back in control as we headed into half-time 3-1 up.

Robert Earnshaw, another former Ram, got himself on the scoresheet after he fired home from close range after good wing play from Nathan Tyson.

Former Forest man Kris Commons pulled a goal back for Derby with a deflected free-kick but it was little consolation as Earnshaw scored again in injury-time to make the final score 5-2.

Tudgay expressed his delight at helping us beat our rivals. He told us: "The game was all about enjoyment and I certainly enjoyed it and I think all the other players on the pitch did too.

"I've played in Derby-Forest games before from my time at Derby so I know what they mean to everyone and especially the fans so we were delighted to have won and now look forward to playing Barnsley next week."

JANUARY

New Year's Day saw us entertain Barnsley at The City Ground, who surprisingly held us to a 2-2 draw.

After going into a shock 2-0 lead through goals from Matt Hill and Andy Gray, it looked as if the Tykes would hold on for all three points.

We showed our strength of character, however, to claim back two goals and take a share of the spoils with Lewis McGugan and Nathan Tyson grabbing our goals.

But we were back to winning ways just two days later, as a Damien Delaney own goal was enough for us to beat Ipswich Town at Portman Road to move us to within two points of the play-offs.

We were on the road again, this time heading to Deepdale to take on struggling Preston in the FA Cup third round.

Despite going behind to a Darren Carter goal, we showed our fighting spirit to overturn the tie with second-half goals from Paul Anderson and Luke Chambers, the latter in injury time, to book our place in the fourth round.

We were back in league action to take on improving Portsmouth where an injury-time Marcus Tudgay header ensured we won the game 2-1.

Kanu had put Pompey in front and we thought we had merely snatched a point through an Ibrahima Sonko own-goal until Tudgay grabbed a late, late winner.

Next up saw us make the short trip along Brian Clough Way to take on rivals Derby at Pride Park.

A goal from substitute Robert Earnshaw saw off the Rams and meant we completed the double over Nigel Clough's men and won for the first time at Pride Park with the win seeing us move into the play-offs.

We continued our impressive unbeaten run by beating Bristol City 1-0 at The City Ground, Chambers adding to his season's tally with another headed goal.

The month ended with defeat, however, as we crashed out of the FA Cup to Premiership West Ham.

Despite defeat, the performance was encouraging but goals from Dele Adebola and David McGoldrick were not enough as Victor Obinna scored a hat-trick.

Before the month ended, we completed the loan signing of England international Paul Konchesky from Liverpool, while Joe Garner joined Scunthorpe on loan.

Tyson showed his delight at completing the double over Derby which saw us retain the Brian Clough trophy.

He said: "To come away with three points here is fantastic, and it was a real solid, nitty-gritty performance.

"It means a lot to all the players, the club and especially the fans."

FEBRUARY

New signing Paul Konchesky went straight into the team upon his arrival and helped us beat Coventry at the Ricoh Arena on his debut.

Goals from Lewis McGugan and Robert Earnshaw were enough for us to do the double over the Sky Blues, despite ex-Red Marlon King giving the home side the lead.

One disappointment from the win was an injury to Guy Moussi which saw the French midfielder miss a large chunk of the season.

We continued our strong form by beating Malky Mackay's Watford 1-0 at The City Ground.

Marcus Tudgay got us off to the perfect start with a goal within 50 seconds and then a dogged defensively display saw us hold on for three points.

This win was followed by a battling point against leaders QPR at Loftus Road, especially considering we played a large part of the game with ten men after Radoslaw Majewski was sent off for a two-footed lunge.

Tommy Smith had put the R's in front but David McGoldrick pulled us level before half time and we held on to take a point from west London.

A similar performance was missing in our next game, however, as we crashed to a 1-0 defeat against Scunthorpe United at Glandford Park.

But we bounced back with a win against promotion rivals Cardiff City at The City Ground to complete a double over the Bluebirds.

Earnshaw scored the winner against his former club after Wes Morgan had given us the lead before Peter Whittingham pulled Cardiff level.

We ended the month with consecutive draws against Preston (home) and Millwall (away).

Konchesky scored his first Forest goal against Preston to cancel out Barry Nicholson's opener for the away side.

Luke Chambers looked as if he had snatched a winner for us in injury-time, but the Lilywhites equalised with the last kick of the game through Billy Jones to take a share of the spoils.

The Millwall game ended goalless at the New Den in a hard-fought encounter.

Morgan spoke about his first goal of the season against Cardiff.

He said: "I'm happy to finally get on the scoresheet and hopefully I can get another before the end of the season

"But overall it was a great result, the manager said we needed a big performance today and thankfully we delivered that."

MARCH

We began the month of March with a trip to Teeside to face Middlesbrough in a rearranged game.

After going behind to a Scott McDonald strike, it looked as though we would leave the north-east with nothing.

That was until big striker Dele Adebola rescued us with an injury-time goal, which he scrambled over the line.

Our joy was shortlived, however, as in the next game we lost our long unbeaten home record when Hull City stunned us at The City Ground.

Matty Fryatt scored the only goal of the game to hand us our first home league defeat since Blackpool beat us way back in September 2009.

The manager Billy Davies responded to this by bringing in highly-rated striker Kris Boyd on loan from Middlesbrough until the end of the season, with reserve keeper Paul Smith going in the opposite direction.

Boyd was named on the bench for the trip to Bramall Lane to play Sheffield United, but he

could do nothing as we slipped to a 2-1 defeat.

Adebola put us in front in the first half but goals after the break from Sam Vokes and Matt Lowton ensured victory for the Blades.

We finished the month with a goalless draw at home to Doncaster Rovers and a 3-2 away defeat to Swansea.

Our goals at the Liberty Stadium were scored by Boyd and Paul Anderson, who enjoyed a loan spell at the Swans earlier in his career, while Scott Sinclair and a brace from on-loan Chelsea man Fabio Borini got the goals for Brendan Rogers' men.

Despite failing to win any of the games in the month we remained in the top six and on course for a place in the play-offs.

Right-back Chris Gunter reflected on the long unbeaten home record after it was ended by Hull.

Said Gunter: "It was always going to end at some point because you can't go on forever.

"It's probably time to look back on it and think what an incredible achievement it was and to go 36 games unbeaten is unbelievable in football nowadays."

APRIL

The first game in April was covered in controversy as Chris Cohen was given a harsh red card against Leeds United at Elland Road.

Cohen was sent off by Mark Halsey when replays showed he clearly took the ball.

The damage was done though as Leeds went on to win the game 4-1 with Garath McCleary scoring our consolation goal with a lovely left-footed finish.

We suffered our third straight defeat against Reading the week after in a very entertaining game at The City Ground.

Ian Harte fired the Royals in front with a fine free-kick before Kris Boyd levelled through a penalty after Lewis McGugan was fouled in the box.

We then went in front through Robert Earnshaw, before Reading hit back just three minutes later with a headed goal from Turkish midfielder Jem Karacan.

Mali international Jimmy Kebe then scored to make it 3-2 to Reading before a foul on Chris Gunter in the box awarded us a penalty with two minutes to go, which McGugan took and confidently fired home.

Reading weren't finished though, and scored a dramatic winner in injury-time thanks to a Luke Chambers' own-goal.

They had the chance to score again, after the referee awarded them a penalty for a handball by Gunter, but Lee Camp saved Shane Long's spot-kick.

The defeat saw us drop to eighth so it was important we got back to winning ways when Burnley visited The City Ground.

We did just that thanks to a late brace from David McGoldrick who had come off the bench. Burnley's Marvin Bartley had earlier been sent off for a high challenge on Chambers.

But we slipped to defeat in the next game away at Norwich in front of the SKY cameras, despite taking the lead through Nathan Tyson.

Tyson chased down a clearance from Norwich stopper John Ruddy, and the ball bounced off the speedy striker and into the net.

The Canaries replied with goals from former Forest striker Grant Holt and midfielder Andrew Surman, while we also had Paul Konchesky sent off in stoppage-time for two bookings.

Yet consecutive 3-2 wins against Leicester City and Bristol City saw us move back into the play-offs.

The goals against Leicester were scored by Marcus Tudgay, Earnshaw and Paul McKenna, and the goals at Ashton Gate were scored by Kris Boyd (two) and Chambers. Robbie Findley also made his first appearances in a Forest shirt in these games since his arrival in January.

We ended the month by thrashing Scunthorpe at the City Ground 5-1, with goals scored by Boyd (two), Chambers (two) and an Anderson strike.

American Robbie Findley revealed his relief at making his Forest debut.

Said Findley: "It took a long time for the injury to heal but it feels good now and I'm just happy that I'm ready to come out and contribute to the team."

MAY

The final month of the season saw us travel to Selhurst Park to finish our season off against Crystal Palace.

Knowing that a point would be enough for us to book our place in the end of season play-offs, we attacked the Eagles straight from kick-off and eventually took the lead through Lewis McGugan.

Palace's Dean Moxey was then sent off for a bad tackle on Marcus Tudgay, before the striker got himself on the score-sheet with a fine header.

Substitute David McGoldrick wrapped up the points with a stunning long-range strike that flew past Speroni and into the top corner.

The win ensured our place in the play-offs and we discovered that we would play Swansea City in the semi-final.

Before the play-off game, it was announced that Luke Chambers had been named our player of the season, while McGugan claimed our goal of the season for his long-range strike against Ipswich Town.

The first play-off leg against the Swans was to be played at home, in front of a sell-out City Ground.

Everything seemed to be going well when Swansea left-back Neil Taylor was shown a straight red card for a high challenge on McGugan in the first minute.

However, we failed to find a breakthrough despite Robert Earnshaw seeing a goal ruled out for offside in the second half.

So the game ended goalless and everything was still to play for in the second leg at the Liberty Stadium four days later.

Despite starting the game the brighter of the two teams, with McGoldrick hitting the bar for us early on, it was the home side who broke the deadlock through Leon Britton who curled a shot past Lee Camp and into the far corner.

Before we had time to react Stephen Dobbie had scored a second for Swansea and we were facing an uphill battle.

Earnshaw did pull a goal back for us late on to halve the deficit and then rattled a post in injury-time that would have sent the tie into extra-time.

With us pressing for the equaliser, goalkeeper Camp joined the attack at a corner but the move backfired when Darren Pratley fired a third for Swansea from long range into the unguarded net to see us suffer play-off heartache for the second season running.

Camp reflected on the season after the play-off defeat to Swansea.

Camp said: "To have had two play-off campaigns in the three years the club has been back in the Championship is something that we can look back on and be very proud of.

"It is a great achievement but it is just frustrating that it has ended in disappointment again."

2010-11 RESULTS

Date	Opponents	Result	Scorers
Sat Aug 7	Burnley	0-1	
Tues Aug 10	Bradford City (CC1)	1-2	Thornhill
Sun Aug 15	LEEDS UNITED	1-1	Blackstock
Sat Aug 21	Reading	1-1	Earnshaw
Sat Aug 28	NORWICH CITY	1-1	Blackstock pen
Sat Sept 11	MILLWALL	1-1	Blackstock
Tues Sept 14	Preston North End	2-1	McGugan 2
Sat Sept 18	Hull City	0-0	
Sat Sept 25	SWANSEA CITY	3-1	McGugan 2 (1 pen), Majewski
Tues Sept 28	SHEFFIELD UNITED	1-1	McKenna
Sat Oct 2	Doncaster Rovers	1-1	Blackstock
Sat Oct 16	Barnsley	1-3	McGugan
Tues Oct 19	MIDDLESBROUGH	1-0	McGugan
Sat Oct 23	IPSWICH TOWN	2-0	McGoldrick, McGugan
Sat Oct 30	Portsmouth	1-2	Anderson
Sat Nov 6	Watford	1-1	McGugan
Tues Nov 9	COVENTRY CITY	2-1	Majewski, Cohen
Sat Nov 13	QUEENS PARK RANGERS	0-0	
Sat Nov 20	Cardiff City	2-0	McGugan, Blackstock
Mon Nov 29	Leicester City	0-1	
Sat Dec 18	CRYSTAL PALACE	3-0	Chambers, Tudgay, McCleary
Wed Dec 29	DERBY COUNTY	5-2	Chambers, Tudgay 2, Earnshaw 2
Sat Jan 1	BARNSLEY	2-2	McGugan pen, Tyson
Mon Jan 3	Ipswich Town	1-0	og (Delaney)
Sat Jan 8	Preston North End (FAC3)	2-1	Anderson, Chambers
Sat Jan 15	PORTSMOUTH	2-1	og (Sonko), Tudgay
Sat Jan 22	Derby County	1-0	Earnshaw
Tues Jan 25	BRISTOL CITY	1-0	Chambers
Sun Jan 30	West Ham United (FAC4)	2-3	Adebola, McGoldrick
Tues Feb 1	Coventry City	2-1	McGugan, Earnshaw
Sat Feb 5	WATFORD	1-0	Tudgay
Sun Feb 13	Queens Park Rangers	1-1	McGoldrick
Wed Feb 16	Scunthorpe United	0-1	
Sat Feb 19	CARDIFF CITY	2-1	Morgan, Earnshaw
Tues Feb 22	PRESTON NORTH END	2-2	Konchesky, Cohen
Sat Feb 26	Millwall	0-0	
Tues Mar 1	Middlesbrough	1-1	Adebola
Sat Mar 5	HULL CITY	0-1	
Tues Mar 8	Sheffield United	1-2	Adebola
Sat Mar 12	DONCASTER ROVERS	0-0	
Sat Mar 19	Swansea City	2-3	Boyd, Anderson
Sat Apr 2	Leeds United	1-4	McCleary
Sat Apr 9	READING	3-4	Boyd pen, Earnshaw, McGugan pen
Tues Apr 12	BURNLEY	2-0	McGoldrick 2
Fri Apr 15	Norwich City	1-2	Tyson
Fr Apr 22	LEICESTER CITY	3-2	Tudgay, Earnshaw, McKenna
Mon Apr 25	Bristol City	3-2	Boyd 2 (1 pen), Chambers
Sat Apr 30	SCUNTHORPE UNITED	5-1	Boyd 2, Chambers 2, Anderson
Sat May 7	Crystal Palace	3-0	McGugan, Tudgay, McGoldrick
Thurs May 12	SWANSEA CITY (P/O SF)	0-0	
Mon May 16	Swansea City (P/O SF)	1-3	Earnshaw

29

SPOT THE DIFFERENCE

Can you spot 8 differences between the pictures below?

Answers on page 61

WHICH COACH AS A YOUTH TEAM PLAYER?

David Joyner. I met him when I was 11 at Northampton Town and he was not only a good coach but he also taught me so much more – including little things like looking people in the eye when you are talking to them and shaking people by the hand when you meet them.

He did so much for me and helped set me on my way towards making a career in the game and it was incredibly sad when he passed away when I was 14.

WHICH FILM?

My favourite film is 'The Matrix' starring Keanu Reeves... but I'm not sure whether you can call it inspirational.

WHICH FAMOUS PERSON?

Ian Wright. I was a big Arsenal fan when I was a kid and he was the main man at that time.

He didn't get into professional football until he was in his 20s and I think his story is quite inspirational.

He had trials with a few clubs when he was a youngster and although he didn't get taken on by them, he is a shining example of someone who didn't give up on his dream.

WHICH BOOK?

I enjoy reading all-action books but I can't think of one that I would say has inspired me.

WHICH PERSON OUTSIDE OF FOOTBALL AS A TEENAGER?

My dad, Les – he did everything he could for me, taking me all over the country when I was a kid trying to make my way in the game.

I wouldn't be where I am now if it hadn't been for his dedication.

WHICH SPORTSPERSON OUTSIDE OF FOOTBALL?

I used to love watching the runner Michael Johnson. He dominated the 200 and 400 metres for a decade and won four Olympic and eight World Championship gold medals along the way. He was just so much better than anyone else and was great to watch.

NOTTINGHAM FOREST 2011-12

Middle Row:
Terry Farndale (Kit Manager) / Daniel Smith
(Assistant Kit Manager) / Jimmy Floyd Hasselbaink
(First Team Coach) / Robbie Findley / Jonathan
Greening / Ben Gathercole / Lee Camp / Paul Smith /
Karl Darlow / Joel Lynch / Guy Moussi / Keith Burt
(Director of Recruitment and Scouting) / Paul Barron
(Goalkeeping Coach) / Zoltan Korpa (Assistant Kit
Manager)

Front Row:
Brendan Moloney / George Boateng / Chris Cohen /
Radoslaw Majewski / Andy Reid / Bill Beswick
(Performance Director) / Steve McClaren (Manager)
/ Rob Kelly (Assistant Manager) / Luke Chambers
/ Paul Anderson / Chris Gunter / Garath McCleary /
Marcus Tudgay

JOIN ROBIN'S

Robin's Reds' membership is available to purchase, so join now and be a part of your favourite team and enjoy exclusive benefits as well.

If you are looking for the best bargain in town, don't look further than Robin's Reds membership.

For just £15 there's a whole range of goodies and opportunities on offer as well as being in pole position to support your favourite football club.

You'll be a member of an exclusive band of young people who have pledged their backing for Steve McClaren and his players as they strive to bring Premier League football back to The City Ground.

And you've a natural-born leader in our mascot Robin Hood, who makes sure that everything is in place for you to enjoy the whole experience of being one of Robin's Reds.

MERRY BAND

The benefits of being a member include the following:

- Exclusive joining pack, including personalised membership card plus special Robin's Reds gifts

- Chance to be a match day mascot*

- Access to exclusive Robin's Reds events

- Priority purchase period for all Forest home and away league games**

- Competitions throughout the season

- Free skate hire at the National Ice Centre***

- Christmas card from the players

  * Subject to age restrictions.

 ** Priority only available subject to availability. To see the priority period on ticket purchases

*** Offer subject to change

How do you join?

You can now join via the Ticket Office, either in person or by calling 0871 226 1980. Calls cost 10p per minute, mobile rates may vary. You can also join online by visiting www.nffcretail.com. If you have a client reference number, use this along with your surname and postcode to log in. If not, ask your mum, dad or guardian to register your details. Once you have joined, we will send your exclusive membership pack out to you in the post along with your personalised membership card. Delivery may take up to 28 days. With your card, you are entitled to:

- Exclusive Robin's Reds events in the new City Ground Megastore

- 10% discount on Forest Coaching Session

- 10% discount on Forest Birthday Parties (Call 0115 982 4453 for details)

Terms and conditions apply.

Robin Hood is not just an heroic outlaw in English folk law but he is also the official Nottingham Forest mascot.

Robin can be seen wandering around The City Ground before Forest matches meeting and greeting all Reds fans young and old.

Join Robin's special 'Robin's Reds' club and be closer to your favourite team.

PLAYER PROFILES

LEE CAMP

Position: Goalkeeper
Birthdate: 22/8/84
Nationality: Northern Irish
Forest Appearances: 117
Forest Goals: 0

The 2010-11 campaign was certainly memorable for Lee – he not only started all 51 of Forest's games and captained The Reds on several occasions but also made his international debut for Northern Ireland.

'Campy' has been the club's most consistent performer since moving to The City Ground from QPR in the summer of 2009 and is widely recognised as the best goalkeeper outside the Premier League.

PAUL SMITH

Position: Goalkeeper
Birthdate: 17/12/79
Nationality: English
Forest Appearances: 140
Forest Goals: 1

Paul has lost his place as Forest's No.1 to Lee Camp but he's ready to play if called upon by manager Steve McClaren.

He went to Middlesbrough on loan for three months of last season and reminded everyone of his talent.

He's famous for having scored a goal after just 23 seconds of a Carling Cup tie against Leicester which is apparently the quickest goal scored by a 'keeper.

KARL DARLOW

Position: Goalkeeper
Birthdate: 8/10/90
Nationality: English
Forest Appearances: 1
Forest Goals: 0

Karl got his big chance in the closing stages of the 2010-11 season when he made his debut for The Reds as a substitute against Crystal Palace.

The youngster has come up through the ranks at The City Ground and now provides cover for Lee Camp and Paul Smith.

Lee rates him very highly and believes he will go on to become a top 'keeper.

CHRIS GUNTER

Position: Right-back
Birthdate: 21/7/89
Nationality: Welsh
Forest Appearances: 102 + 4
Forest Goals: 1

The Welsh international has been a Forest regular since joining the club from Tottenham in the summer of 2009 after a successful loan at The City Ground.

He started his career with Cardiff and quickly earned a big reputation, leading to him making his senior international debut at the age of 17.

As well as being a top-class defender he is also well known for his speedy raids down the right flank and can also play at left-back.

* Statistics correct to end of 2010-11 season.

BRENDAN MOLONEY

Position: Right-back
Birthdate: 18/1/89
Nationality: Irish
Forest Appearances: 18 + 5
Forest Goals: 0

Brendan has played most of his football in recent years away from The City Ground in loan spells with Chesterfield, Notts County and Scunthorpe.

But he forced his way back into the Forest first-team in the closing stages of last season and produced a string of eye-catching displays.

He is a Republic of Ireland Under-21 international who has been on Forest's books since he was a schoolboy.

JOEL LYNCH

Position: Central defender or left-back
Birthdate: 3/10/87
Nationality: English
Forest Appearances: 43 + 8
Forest Goals: 0

One of the most versatile players in the Forest squad, Joel can play in a number of defensive positions.

He has been unfortunate with injuries since moving to The City Ground from Brighton in the summer of 2009 but never lets the team down when he gets an opportunity.

Joel was still a youth-team player when he made his debut for Brighton in 2006 and made more than 80 appearances for The Seagulls before joining The Reds.

LUKE CHAMBERS

Position: Central defender
Birthdate: 28/9/85
Nationality: English
Forest Appearances: 162 + 20
Forest Goals: 19

The 2010-11 campaign was a personal triumph for Luke as he established himself in his favourite position in the centre of defence and was named Player of the Year by our supporters.

He also bagged an impressive seven goals, including the opener in the memorable 5-2 win over arch-rivals Derby.

'Chambo' started his career with Northampton, where he made his debut as a 17 year-old, before joining Forest in 2007. A natural leader, he can also play at right-back.

WES MORGAN

Position: Central defender
Birthdate: 21/1/84
Nationality: English
Forest Appearances: 359 + 19
Forest Goals: 12

Wes is Forest's longest-serving player – he made his debut for the club in 2003 – and is also one of the most popular with supporters.

He played in all 51 of Forest's games last season and formed a hugely impressive partnership at the heart of the defence with Luke Chambers.

Started his career with Notts County but went to college after leaving Meadow Lane. Forest spotted him playing for a local team and he has hardly looked back since.

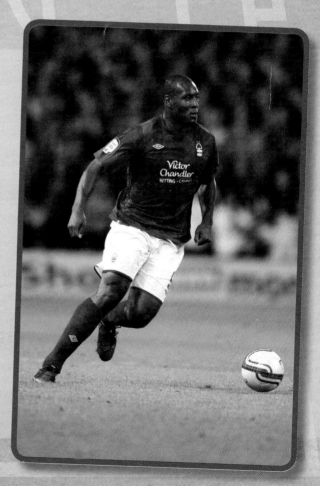

PLAYER PROFILES

CHRIS COHEN

Position: Midfielder

Birthdate: 5/3/87

Nationality: English

Forest Appearances: 189 + 2

Forest Goals: 13

He has been a model of consistency since joining Forest from Yeovil in the summer of 2007 and has established himself as a key figure at The City Ground.

An all-action player, he was voted Player of the Year in 2009 and enhanced his reputation last season as a gifted performer with a string of outstanding displays.

Chris, who started his career with West Ham, can also play at left-back but much prefers to occupy a midfield role.

RADOSLAW MAJEWSKI

Position: Midfielder

Birthdate: 15/12/86

Nationality: Polish

Forest Appearances: 60 + 10

Forest Goals: 6

The Polish international will be hoping to play a more prominent role at The City Ground this season after starting less than half of Forest's games last term.

But with his twinkling skills and ability to spot a pass he's still one of the most talented performers at the disposal of The Reds.

'Radi' originally joined Forest on loan from Polonia Warsaw in 2009 but that deal was made permanent a year later after he took English football by storm in his first season.

LEWIS McGUGAN

Position: Midfielder
Birthdate: 25/10/88
Nationality: English
Forest Appearances: 115 + 43
Forest Goals: 31

He's one of the most talented midfielders outside the Premier League, as he showed last season by topping Forest's scoring charts with 13 goals.

Long-range goals are his speciality and his spectacular 35-yard free-kick against Ipswich was voted Goal of the Season by Forest fans.

A local lad, he joined The Reds as a schoolboy and has worked his way up through the ranks. Lewis has also represented England at various youth levels.

PAUL ANDERSON

Position: Winger
Birthdate: 23/7/88
Nationality: English
Forest Appearances: 94 + 19
Forest Goals: 11

Paul is no stranger to success as he was a member of the Liverpool side that won the FA Youth Cup in 2006 and two years later helped Swansea to the League One title.

He was on loan at Swansea and had a similar spell with Forest before joining The Reds on a permanent basis in 2009.

One of the quickest wingers in the Championship, he started 30 games last season and bagged four goals.

GARATH McCLEARY

Position: Winger

Birthdate: 15/5/87   **Nationality:** English

Forest Appearances: 30 + 70   **Forest Goals:** 4

Garath will be hoping to start games on a more regular basis this season after he only made eight league and cup starts last term.

But the lively winger still showed glimpses of his vast potential, particularly with a spectacular goal against Leeds at Elland Road.

After several years in non-league football he got his big break in 2008 when Forest snapped him up from Bromley after a successful trial.

DEXTER BLACKSTOCK

Position: Striker

Birthdate: 20/5/86   **Nationality:** English

Forest Appearances: 57 + 14   **Forest Goals:** 21

Dexter is still recovering from the horrific knee injury he suffered against Cardiff in November 2010 that put his career on hold.

But he's making good progress and hopes it won't be too long before he's back doing what he does best - scoring goals.

He started his career with Southampton and joined Forest from QPR in 2009 after helping The Reds avoid relegation during a highly successful loan spell. He has also played for England's Under-21 side.

MATT DERBYSHIRE

Position: Striker

Birthdate: 14/04/86   **Nationality:** English

Forest Appearances: 0   **Forest Goals:** 0

After a spell in Greek football with Olympiakos, the former England Under-21 striker jumped at the chance to join Steve McClaren's City Ground recruitment drive in August 2011.

He spent much of his earlier career with Blackburn Rovers and after loan spells with Plymouth and Wrexham joined Olympiakos under a similar arrangement.

So successful was that move that he signed permanently for the Greek club until a change in the club's manager left him looking back to England to reassert himself.

ISHMAEL MILLER

Birthdate: 05/03/87

Position: Striker   **Nationality:** English

Forest Appearances: 0   **Forest Goals:** 0

The big striker was Steve McClaren's fifth signing after his appointment, joining the club from West Brom in an initial £1.2m transfer.

He began his career with Manchester City and made 17 league appearances for them before signing for West Brom in a permanent deal that followed a successful loan spell at The Hawthorns.

Injury prevented him making a bigger contribution in the west Midlands and he had an extended loan with Queens Park Rangers, helping them into the Premier League as winners of the Championship in 2011.

MARCUS TUDGAY

Position: Striker

Birthdate: 3/2/83   **Nationality:** English

Forest Appearances: 20 + 4   **Forest Goals:** 7

Marcus made a dream start to his Forest career after moving to The City Ground from Sheffield Wednesday in November 2010.

He scored on his debut against Crystal Palace and followed that up with two goals in his next game against his former club Derby County.

He almost joined Forest as a schoolboy but started his career with Derby and scored 17 goals in 92 league appearances for The Rams.

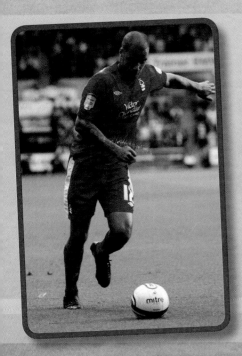

DAVID McGOLDRICK

Position: Striker

Birthdate: 29/11/87   **Nationality:** English

Forest Appearances: 32 + 32   **Forest Goals:** 9

He returned home when he joined Forest from Southampton in 2009 having been born in Nottingham and started his career with Notts County.

David is still waiting to establish himself as a first-team regular at The City Ground but has made vital contributions for the team, including both goals in a 2-0 win over Burnley last season.

He was still at school when he made his first-team debut for County and was snapped up by Southampton after making just 10 appearances for The Magpies.

ANDY REID

Position: Midfielder

Birthdate: 29/07/82   **Nationality:** Irish

Forest Appearances: 135 + 25   **Forest Goals:** 25

The Republic of Ireland international became Steve McClaren's first signing as Forest manager in July 2011.

He started his career with The Reds but joined Tottenham in 2005 and has also played in the Premier League for Charlton, Sunderland and Blackpool.

JOE GARNER

Position: Striker

Birthdate: 12/04/88   **Nationality:** English

Forest Appearances: 34 + 17   **Forest Goals:** 10

After loan spells with Huddersfield Town and Scunthorpe United in the 2010-11 season, the Lancashire-born striker is looking to make his mark on the Forest scene.

He was signed from Carlisle in July 2008 in a deal worth over £1m but has had to move on loan deals in order to add to his experience. He began his career with his local side Blackburn Rovers but moved to Carlisle in January 2007 in search of regular first-team football.

JONATHAN GREENING

Position: Midfielder

Birthdate: 2/01/79   **Nationality:** English

Forest Appearances: 0   **Forest Goals:** 0

The vastly experienced star quit the Premier League to join Forest in July 2011 after the club paid Fulham an undisclosed fee for his services.

He worked with Steve McClaren at Manchester United and Middlesbrough and admitted the chance to link up with him again was a key factor in his decision to sign a three-year contract at The City Ground.

GUY MOUSSI

Position: Midfielder

Birthdate: 23/01/85   **Nationality:** French

Forest Appearances: 79   **Forest Goals:** 3

The popular Frenchman delighted Forest fans when he signed a new three-year contract in the summer of 2011.

His existing deal had expired and there were fears he would leave amid interest from a host of other clubs but Moussi opted to stay at The City Ground and has his sights set on helping Forest reach the Premier League.

ROBBIE FINDLEY

Position: Striker

Birthdate: 4/08/85   **Nationality:** American

Forest Appearances: 0 + 2   **Forest Goals:** 0

Luck deserted Robbie after he joined Forest in January as he picked up a thigh injury in his first training session with the club.

He was restricted to just two substitute appearances last season and will be hoping to make up for lost time.

A lightning-quick player, he made his name in the American MLS with Real Salt Lake and appeared in three of the US's games at the 2010 World Cup finals.

GEORGE BOATENG

Position: Midfielder

Birthdate: 5/09/75   **Nationality:** Dutch

Forest Appearances: 0   **Forest Goals:** 0

The vastly experienced star has played for four clubs in the Premier League – Coventry, Aston Villa, Middlesbrough, where he worked under Steve McClaren, and Hull – and has also represented his country, Holland.

He joined Forest during the summer of 2011, signing a one-year contract, after a spell in Greek football with Skoda Xanthi.

WORDSEARCH

15 players, managers and football terms are hidden in the grid below – can you find them?

F	M	A	S	C	O	T	N	A	G	R	O	M	R
C	C	E	M	A	T	U	M	K	B	I	O	D	E
L	G	H	N	T	Y	D	N	I	Y	A	W	E	D
F	U	C	B	E	H	G	Z	X	C	U	L	B	S
I	G	T	B	S	L	A	T	H	L	F	D	L	R
E	A	I	C	I	T	Y	G	R	O	U	N	D	O
O	N	P	T	J	G	R	A	Q	U	D	W	R	B
D	U	G	O	U	T	L	E	K	G	O	E	F	I
N	E	R	A	L	C	C	M	N	H	S	I	M	N
C	H	A	M	B	E	R	S	T	T	J	F	W	S
S	R	W	P	O	U	W	Q	T	S	E	R	O	F

Mascot   Robin   Clough
Ditch   Ball   McGovern
Nigg   Brent   Dugout
Forest   McGugan   Chambers
McClaren   Widgey   Morgan

Answers on page 61

46

FOREST LEGEND

ROY KEANE

Roy Keane became one of the world's top midfielders in a distinguished career spent largely at Manchester United.

But the boy from Cork might never have gone on to put his name in Old Trafford lights had he not been discovered by our scouting staff in the summer of 1990.

Keane was playing for Cobh Ramblers at the time when he was given the opportunity of joining The City Ground playing staff.

But within months he was making a baptism of fire in English football when he played for us against Liverpool at Anfield in August 1990.

Hardly anyone in the ground that night had even heard of Roy Keane but that did not remain the case for long as the Irish star's career developed at an impressive pace.

We lost the Liverpool game 2-0 but a star was born and Keane went on to play a leading role in Brian Clough's team that reached the FA Cup final in his first year with us. He also played for us in the 1992 League Cup final when we were beaten 1-0 by Manchester United.

He won recognition for the Republic of Ireland national side during his time with us and he went on to play 154 games and score 33 goals at The City Ground.

When his days at United ended he went on to play for Celtic and then managed Sunderland and Ipswich.

TOP 10 GOALSCORERS
FOREST

GRENVILLE MORRIS
217 GOALS

Our all-time leading goalscorer, Gren had tremendous patience in front of goal, remaining calm when a chance fell at his feet. His laid-back attitude and consistency saw him net 217 times in the 457 games he played with Forest. With five hat-tricks to his name and top scorer in seven out of ten seasons he spent with the club, Gren's record will take some beating.

NIGEL CLOUGH
131 GOALS

'The Number 9' as he was referred to by his dad, Nigel scored an impressive 131 goals for the Reds. Nigel was the club's leading scorer in four successive seasons during 1985-89, when we won back-to-back League Cups. Clough forged many lethal striking partners during his time at the club, including with the likes of Peter Davenport, Garry Birtles and Lee Chapman.

WALLY ARDRON
124 GOALS

In terms of goals-to-games ratio, Walter or 'Wally' as he was known was the most prolific marksman the club has seen, scoring an incredible 124 goals in 191 appearances. He was a superstar in his day, a dynamic centre-forward breaking records wherever he played. During 1949-53 Ardron topped our scoring chart, bagging six hat tricks – a club record which still stands to this day.

JOHNNY DENT
122 GOALS

As an old-fashioned style centre-forward, Dent was a popular figure for the Reds in the 1930s. His workmanlike never-say-die attitude and hard graft earned him a scoring record which bettered a goal in every other game. His partnership with Tom Peacock saw them both net over 100 goals before Dent departed for Kidderminster Harriers.

IAN STOREY-MOORE
118 GOALS

Storey-Moore built a reputation as a fast, direct and inspirational figure for Forest during 1962-72. Before securing a high profile move to Manchester United, he scored an impressive 118 goals for the Reds. He was a cult hero at The City Ground but sadly his career was cut short following his move to Old Trafford because of a persistent ankle injury.

ENOCH WEST
100 GOALS

Enoch 'Knocker' West bagged a century of goals for both Forest and Manchester United. In the early 20th century he helped Forest gain promotion into the top flight with his powerful no-nonsense style of play. Knocker will be forever etched into the club's history books as he scored a hat-trick during our all-time biggest win against Leicester Fosse – a 12-0 win in 1909.

GARRY BIRTLES
96 GOALS

Long Eaton-born and bred, Garry came from non-league football to reach European glory during his time at the club. Birtles, along with strike-partners Tony Woodcock and Trevor Francis, helped the Reds secure back-to-back European Cup titles as well as a League Cup and Super Cup winners' medal. His clinical finishing and tireless workrate were prominent features in his all-round game.

JOHN ROBERTSON
95 GOALS

Scottish international Robertson scored a valuable 95 goals with us during his time at the club. A player more renowned for creating

goals than scoring, 'Robbo's' finest moment came when he scored the winning goal in the European Cup final against Hamburg in 1980. His knack of scoring important goals was never better illustrated than his unerring accuracy form the penalty spot.

TOMMY WILSON
89 GOALS

At the beginning of his career, Wilson struggled to cement a regular first-team place with us. However, as strikers came and went, Tommy found his shooting boots and began to consistently score goals. His most valuable contribution came when he scored the winning goal in the 2-1 victory over Luton Town in the 1959 FA Cup final. He improved with age and when his Forest career came to an end in 1960 Wilson had scored an average of almost one goal in every two games.

IAN BOWYER
96 GOALS

Ian enjoyed two successful spells with us in the 70s and 80s in a marvellous career lasting 23 years. The hard-working midfielder scored 97 goals with the Reds before going on to football management with Hereford. Ian created football history when he played in the same Hereford side as his son, Gary and in later years was Paul Hart's No. 2 at The City Ground.

NOTTINGHAM FOREST ALL-TIME TOP TEN GOALSCORERS

	Name	Played	Goals
1	Grenville Morris	1898-1913	217
2	Nigel Clough	1984-1997	131
3	Wally Ardron	1949-1955	124
4	Johnny Dent	1929-1936	122
5	Storey-Moore	1963-1972	118
6	Enoch West	1905-1910	100
7	Garry Birtles	1976-1987	96
8	Ian Bowyer	1973-1987	96
9	John Robertson	1970-1986	95
10	Tommy Wilson	1951-1960	89

PLAYER OF THE YEAR

Luke Chambers always was a fans' favourite at The City Ground – and now it's been confirmed with silverware.

The reliable defender followed some illustrious names from our history when he was named Player of the Year for 2010-11.

And he was thrilled to bits, knowing that the award came as a result of a supporters' poll.

He admitted: "I like to think I've always had a great relationship with the fans – even when things were not going quite so well for me.

"But last season the support I got was tremendous and I can't thank everyone enough for their backing and also for voting for me in the poll.

"When I took the trophy home for the first time my girlfriend and I were looking at the names of the past winners and for me to be named alongside the likes of Stuart Pearce and Des Walker is unbelievable.

"They – and others – were legends in the club's history and I wouldn't pretend for one second that I am in that kind of bracket.

"But it gave me enormous pride to receive the award and I'm sure it gave a lot of people who are close to me a lot of pleasure too.

"I know my parents were delighted about it all. They have supported me from being a young lad kicking a ball about and my dad still travels all over the country watching me play."

Chambers celebrated the award by scoring twice in our last home match of the Championship season against Scunthorpe United when we virtually secured a play-off spot.

But, like all his teammates, he was bitterly disappointed that they just missed out on a place in the Premier League

He added: "It was all very disappointing really, particularly after we had reached the play-offs the previous season as well.

"We found some good form towards the end of the season and were hoping that we could take that into the games against Swansea but unfortunately we didn't quite do it.

"We tried everything we could to turn things our way at Swansea but at the end of the day we had to accept it wasn't going to be our year.

"All it did was make us all the more determined to do well again this season and let's hope this time it is very much a case of third time lucky."

FOREST MAZE

Can you help Robin find his way through the maze?

START

FINISH

MY INSPIRATIONS
LEWIS McGUGAN

WHICH COACH AS A YOUTH TEAM PLAYER?

Chris Dowhan who coached me for four years from Under-10 level onwards at Forest. He was the person who spotted that I had above-average ability and convinced me that I was good enough to make a career in the game. He's one of the best coaches I've ever worked with... if not the best!

WHICH PERSON OUTSIDE OF FOOTBALL AS A TEENAGER?

My brothers Curtis and Jermaine. They were both better footballers than me when I was growing up but unfortunately didn't get the chance to make a career for themselves in the game.

But even though that was a huge disappointment for them both they supported me and made sure I didn't do anything stupid that might have ruined my chances of making it.

WHICH MANAGER?

I would have to say Colin Calderwood because he was the manager who gave me my big opportunity at Forest.

Who knows what might have happened if it hadn't been for him? I probably wouldn't be where I am now and I'm grateful to him for showing faith in me.

WHICH FILM?

My favourite film is 'John Q' starring Denzel Washington. I don't really know why I like it so much – perhaps it's because it is based on a true story about a father trying to do the best he can for his poorly son.

WHICH SPORTSPERSON OUTSIDE OF FOOTBALL?

Golfer Tiger Woods. I enjoy playing golf and although I'm gradually getting better I'm in awe of the top players and just how good they are.

When he was at his peak, Tiger was virtually untouchable and it's hard to believe that one man could have dominated a sport for so long.

53

GOAL OF THE SEASON

Such was the quality of his strikes last season that Lewis McGugan almost had a 'Goal of the Season' competition all of his own.

But one of his 13 goals stood out from the rest and in the end his cracker against Ipswich Town at The City Ground in October won the award by a landslide.

It was an audacious attempt in the first place and as he lined up a potential strike from 35 yards, teammate Chris Cohen is reported to have announced: "If he puts this in I'm going home!"

But, with a bit of encouragement from the bench, our midfielder made up his mind to try his luck and left Ipswich goalkeeper Martin Fullop grasping at thin air as the ball arrowed into the top corner.

Said Lewis: "It was only a couple of minutes before half-time and we were already a goal up through David McGoldrick.

"I knew it was a long way out but there wasn't much time left on the clock and I got a shout from the bench 'to let one go'.

"As soon as it left my right boot I knew I had connected well but I didn't expect it to end up in the top corner like it did.

"Everyone said it would be the goal of the season but it was in October and we scored a lot of goals after that.

"I'm sure it did look spectacular and it is the kind of strike I was very pleased with – I just hope I can repeat it at some stage in the future.

"But to be honest it was one of those freak things that did everything you hoped it would. They only come along once in a blue moon.

"At the end of the season I was naturally delighted and proud to collect the award. It's good to collect any award, particularly when supporters vote for you."

So what makes Lewis such a threat from deadball situations?

He revealed: "I do practise striking the ball correctly when I can but you don't try and find the corners of the net.

"All I focus on is getting a clean hit and then trying to make sure I hit the target. The balls in the modern game can do all sorts of things and if you make sure you give the goalkeeper something to do, you never know what it might lead to.

"It's frightening how much movement there is in these balls at times so goalkeepers can spill them or, on those occasions like the one against Ipswich, they can fly into the top corner.

"But the coaching staff are always on to us about hitting the target and making goalkeepers work. That's the biggest requirement of all."

Lewis's wonder goal against the Tractor Boys also proved to be good news for one of our fans, Dave Abbiss, who won himself a laptop computer on the strength of it.

Dave was one of our fans who voted for the effort as the 'Goal of the Season' and of all those who did so, his name was picked out of the hat for the prize donated by one of our Associate Directors, Graham Cartledge.

BOB MCKINLAY
(1951-1969)

An outstanding centre-half who was regarded as one of the gentlemanly figures in the game. He was born in Lochgelly and was reckoned to be one of the best defenders never to be capped by Scotland. He had an amazing run of 265 consecutive league appearances for us but his finest hour came as a member of our 1959 FA Cup final-winning team. He also captained us in the last five years of his career.

IAN BOWYER
(1973-1987)

The tough tackling, no-nonsense midfielder was an ever-dependable figure during the club's European glory years of the late 70's. Ian was a workaholic, a grafter and scorer of vital goals during his 20 years in the game. After a brief spell at Sunderland Ian ('Bomber', as he was always known) returned to Forest in 1982 for a second time and went on to make 541 appearances scoring 96 goals.

STUART PEARCE
1985-1997

Signed by Brian Clough in 1985, Pearce went on to spend 12 successful years at the club. A crowd favourite, 'Psycho' became known worldwide for his passion and desire to win both for club and country. His thunderbolt of a left foot helped him score 88 times in 522 matches for the Reds, tremendous return for a left back. After being bought by Cloughie for a mere £200,000 Stuart was a great competitor and a true leader.

STEVE CHETTLE
1987-2000

The local lad made good was a steady, calm and composed centre back and someone to rely on in times of pressure. His ability to pass the ball out of defence suited Forest's style and helped the club win several trophies during his era. Arguably his finest moment came when he scored for the Reds in the UEFA Cup against Bayern Munich in Germany.

JOHN ROBERTSON
1970-1986

Robbo was a wing wizard who could turn a match on its head with his trickery and deceptive pace. His appearance was scruffy and he often looked overweight but Robbo's creative talents and goals helped Forest achieve unprecedented levels of domestic and European success. His superb individual goal against Hamburg in the 1980 European Cup final earned the Reds their second consecutive European title.

GEOFF THOMAS
1944-1960

Right back Thomas was a vital member of the Forest team that won the Third Division title in 1951. In an injury-plagued career, Geoff missed out on the opportunity to play in the 1959 FA Cup final against Luton. It is thought he would have made many more appearances had the fixtures not been constantly interrupted by the effects of the war.

JACK BURKITT
1948-1961

Originally a centre half, Jack earned a reputation as a consistent old fashioned wing half. Captaining the 1959 FA Cup winning side and helping the club to two successful promotion campaigns, Jack will be remembered for his determination and dedication to the club. In later years he was on the club's coaching staff and also managed our neighbours Notts County.

VIV ANDERSON
1974-1984

Viv was a prodigy of the Forest youth policy. As an attacking full-back 'Spider' was a key figure during the European Cup glory days. He earned his status as the first black footballer to win a full England cap and went on to make 30 international appearances for his country. He also played for Manchester United, Arsenal and Sheffield Wednesday before finishing his playing career at Barnsley.

JACK ARMSTRONG
1905-1922

Jack proved a useful utility player for the Reds, playing in every outfield position between 1905 and 1922. His favoured position, however, was wing-half where his quick footwork and turn of pace proved a handful for most defences. Had it not been for the WW1 Jack would surely have gone on to appear well over 500 times for Forest.

GRENVILLE MORRIS
1989-1913

Top scorer in seven out of the 10 seasons spent with the club, Grenville scored five hat-tricks during his time with the Reds. The Welsh international – he won his first cap at the age of 18 - was later known as the 'immortal Gren' due to his incredible fitness regime and 100 per cent commitment. He was also a very fine tennis player.

NOTTINGHAM FOREST ALL-TIME TOP TEN APPEARANCES

1	Bob McKinlay	1951-1969	682/3
2	Ian Bowyer	1973-1987	541/23
3	Steve Chettle	1987-2000	503/23
4	Stuart Pearce	1985-1997	522
5	John Robertson	1970-1986	499/15
6	Jack Burkitt	1948-1961	503
7	Jack Armstrong	1905-1922	460
8	Grenville Morris	1898-1913	460
9	Geoff Thomas	1944- 1960	431
10	Viv Anderson	1974- 1984	425/5

MUNICH FINAL

We had our finest hour in the German city of Munich in 1979 when we won the European Cup for the first time by beating Swedish champions Malmo in the final.

The memorable victory came courtesy of a headed goal by football's first £1m man Trevor Francis, who converted a cross by John Robertson to give us a 1-0 win.

It was a very special day in Francis's marvellous career – not least because he wasn't sure of playing in the game.

He said: "I was cup-tied right up until the final and although I was hoping I would be selected, I wasn't sure until the manager named the team.

"I felt as though I was fortunate in many ways but I've never felt so much pressure going into a game because I felt I had to justify the manager's faith in me.

"I felt I did that by getting the winning goal and it was a wonderful feeling."

Although the final itself was disappointing as a game, we had overcome many major hurdles to get there – not least defeating reigning English

and European champions Liverpool in the very first round.

We went on to defeat AEK Athens, Grasshoppers Zurich and German champions Cologne to qualify for the final that saw our fans turn Munich into a sea of red and white.

And those fans were back in Nottingham city centre soon afterwards to welcome their heroes home and celebrate the greatest moment in the club's history.

MADRID FINAL

Not satisfied with winning the European Cup on one occasion, we went on to retain the magnificent trophy the following year.

This time John Robertson, who made the crucial goal 12 months before, was creator turned goalscorer when his right footed shot proved good enough to beat top German side Hamburg in the Madrid final.

But the 1-0 victory owed as much to the grit and determination of an injury-hit side as Robertson's match-winning goal.

Even now Robertson still has special memories of that night in the Spanish capital. He said: "I remember shouting 'goal' and then being mobbed by the rest of the lads. I just stood there with my arms in the air unable to move.

"It was an unbelievable experience and one that very few players are fortunate to have in their careers.

"We had to defend for long periods but we defended magnificently as a team and the longer the game went on the more and more confident we felt about winning the trophy for a second time."

We went into the game without Trevor Francis but teenager Gary Mills came into the side to play his part in another unbelievable episode in our great history.

To win the European Cup once was a tremendous achievement for Brian Clough, Peter Taylor and the players but to win it twice in successive years was simply fantastic.

On our way to the final we had defeated Swedish side Oesters Vaxjo, Rumanian champions Arges Pitesti, Dynamo Berlin and the past European masters of Ajax.

QUIZ ANSWERS

WHO AM I? Page 12

Wes Morgan

Marcus Tudgay

Luke Chambers

Garath McCleary

FOREST QUIZ Page 16

1 Lewis McGugan

2 Tottenham Hotspur

3 Wes Morgan

4 Martin O'Neill

5 Dave Bassett

6 Lee Camp and Wes Morgan

7 Robert Earnshaw 2, Marcus Tudgay, Luke Chambers

8 Andy Reid

9 Jack Lester

10 Middlesbrough

11 QPR, Norwich, Swansea, Cardiff, Reading

12 Real Salt Lake

13 The Executive Stand

14 Yeovil

15 Chris Cohen

16 West Brom, Hull, Liverpool

17 Dexter Blackstock

18 Derby County

19 Eighteen

20 Dele Adebola and David McGoldrick

SPOT THE DIFFERENCE Page 30

WORDSEARCH Page 46

F	M	A	S	C	O	T	N	A	G	R	O	M	R
C	C	E	M	A	T	U	M	K	B	I	O	D	E
L	G	H	N	T	Y	D	N	I	Y	A	W	E	D
F	U	C	B	E	H	G	Z	X	C	U	L	B	S
I	G	T	B	S	L	A	T	H	L	F	D	L	R
E	A	I	C	I	T	Y	G	R	O	U	N	D	O
O	N	P	T	J	G	R	A	Q	U	D	W	R	B
D	U	G	O	U	T	L	E	K	G	O	E	F	I
N	E	R	A	L	C	C	M	N	H	S	I	M	N
C	H	A	M	B	E	R	S	T	T	J	F	W	S
S	R	W	P	O	U	W	Q	T	S	E	R	O	F

WHERE'S
ROBIN?
EXIT ➔ 12
Victor Chandler
COME ON YOU RED
EMERGENCY EXIT
SPORTS
Hickling&Squires
The Money